J̶ and Joan Toad

by Josh Weinstein
illustrations by Steve Royal

Harcourt Brace & Company

Orlando Atlanta Austin Boston San Francisco Chicago Dallas New York Toronto London

Jo Frog and Joan Toad always played together. But Joan Toad liked to swim . . .

and Jo Frog didn't.
"It's so cold," Jo Frog told
Joan Toad.

One day, Joan Toad chose a hole to swim in. "Let's go, Jo!" Joan croaked, and dove right in.

Joan Toad floated down into the hole.
"Oh, no," groaned Jo Frog.
"Where did Joan go?"

Jo Frog poked a pole into the hole. "Help!" moaned Joan Toad as she grabbed the pole. "I'm so cold!"

But Joan Toad couldn't hold on to the pole. "Help!" Joan moaned and groaned.

Jo Frog found a hose, but it broke on a stone. Jo tossed in a rope, but it floated away from Joan Toad.

"I'm so cold," croaked Joan.
"Get me out of this hole!"

So Jo Frog tied one end of another rope to a post. And Jo dove into the hole to take the other end to Joan.

Jo Frog towed Joan Toad out of the hole. "Oh, Jo!" groaned Joan. "I was so cold, I almost froze!"

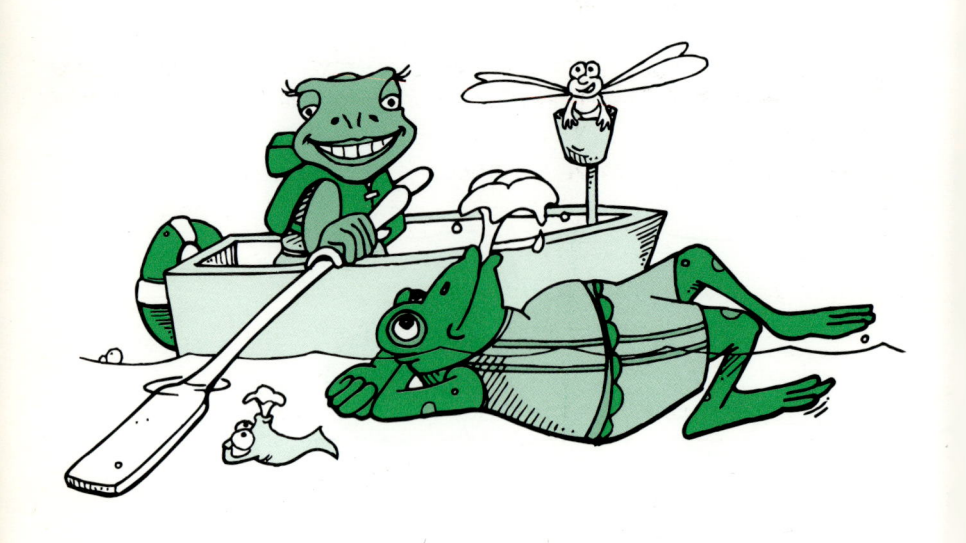

Now Jo Frog swims all the time. And Joan Toad still goes into holes—but only in a boat and only if Jo is close!